Emotional Intelligence

A Beginner's Guide to Understanding Emotions, Raising Your EQ and Improving Your Self-Knowledge

NEAL D. ROSCHMANN

liable for any hardship or damages that may befall them after undertaking information described herein.

Additionally, the information in the following pages is intended only for informational purposes and should thus be thought of as universal. As befitting its nature, it is presented without assurance regarding its prolonged validity or interim quality. Trademarks that are mentioned are done without written consent and can in no way be considered an endorsement from the trademark holder.

Table of Contents

Introduction

Congratulations on downloading *Emotional Intelligence: A Beginner's Guide to Understanding Emotions, Raising Your EQ and Improving Your Self-Knowledge* and thank you for doing so.

The following chapters will discuss valuable ways you can uncover your true intentions and begin to live a life full of purpose. The gems listed below are meant to be practical applications you can apply to your daily life. It is our hope that you finish this book with the essential tools needs to assist with living to your fullest potential!

There are plenty of books on this subject on the market, thanks again for choosing this one! Every effort was made to ensure it is full of as much useful information as possible, please enjoy!

Chapter 1: Understanding Your Strengths and Weaknesses

"Mastering Others is Strength. Mastering Yourself Is True Power."-Lao Tzu

Superheroes are revered throughout the world for being immensely powerful and possessing great strength. Whether it's the unapologetic charisma portrayed by Batman or the indestructible might that is Superman, they all are known for their unique strengths. As iconic as these fictional heroes are, they are endowed with the daunting presence of a weakness. Sure, Spiderman can extract web shooters from his body and conquer extreme heights. However, the paralyzing guilt concerning the

death of his uncle ate young Peter Parker alive.

Although we may not have superhuman strength or genetic mutations, we all own a personal list of strengths and weaknesses that make us unique. In movies and books, the hero is only able to reach optimal enlightenment once he or she unveils the root of their weakness. Similarly, we encounter challenging situations daily that require us to utilize our strengths and destroy our weaknesses.

When contemplating a future career, one of the main components of the interviewing process is establishing what your greatest strengths are. Many list general qualities such as reliability, technical skills, or effective communication. While those are all valuable assets to any team, they are surface level descriptions.

When meeting someone new for the first time, naturally you would want to emphasize your greatest qualities. Trustworthiness, loyalty, and the ability to be kind are all examples of surface level strengths on a personal level. Understanding your strengths and weaknesses involves an intuitive look at your personality. This involves analyzing the self in a deep manner.

How Can I Accomplish This?

Abraham Maslow is one of the founding fathers of positive psychology. He established a hierarchy of needs that works as a mirror of the self. The pyramid begins with basic, instinctual needs and evolves into higher actualization. Reaching this nirvana of self-actualization isn't as complex as it may seem. In fact, you can begin your journey to understanding yourself immediately! Let's consider a few personal questions that will help you to correctly identify your strengths and weaknesses.

What Set's You Apart?

Look around at your network of associates and compare your traits to theirs. Is there a specific quality about yourself that makes you unique? Each person in a network brings different strengths to the table that complement the relationship. Some valuable questions to ask yourself are:

- Are you a great listener?

- Do your friends often come to you to solve problems?

- Are you awesome at getting the party started?

- Do you make others feel warm and comfortable?

By analyzing your role in comparison to others, you will find where your strengths lie.

What Excites You?

That little jump of excitement that occurs when you are engaging in a specific activity is what moves you. The beauty in excitement surrounding tasks is that it doesn't happen often. When it does occur, that feeling stands out. Pay attention and make note of what gets your blood going. There has to be some spark that motivates you to wake up in the morning. Ralph Waldo Emerson once quoted, *"Enthusiasm is one of the most powerful engines of success. When you do a thing, do it with all your might. Put your whole soul into it. Stamp it with your own personality. Be active, be energetic, be enthusiastic and faithful, and you will accomplish your object. Nothing great was ever achieved without enthusiasm."*

What's Holding You Back?

Being stagnant will pause any hope of finding new strengths. If you engage in the same activities without pushing yourself, you will never know what you are truly capable of. A 1998 study found that 40 female participants were more fearful of anticipated pain as opposed to pain already felt. [1] This study proved the notion that we inherently fear what is foreign to us, which inhibits our ability to try new things. Naturally so, the unknown can be filled with scary monsters. However, the unknown could also be filled with inspirational fairies waiting to fulfill our wishes. Explore different experiences and push yourself out of your comfort zone. By doing so, you will discover new qualities about yourself that you never knew existed. A few new activities to try are:

1. Pursuing a new job role will help you to discover new areas of expertise.

2. Take up a new hobby such as painting or knitting. These activities require patience and attention to detail. These may be new outlets that could reveal new talents.

3. Enroll in a new class. Many online platforms offer free classes that cover a variety of subjects from computer science to photography.

4. Read valuable books that will enlighten your mind and perspective on foreign topics.

---

[1] Arntz, Arnoud; Hopmans, Miranda (1998): Under-predicted Pain Disrupts More than Correctly Predicted Pain, But Does Not Hurt More

5. Embark on a new adventure; try hiking, rock climbing or running. These will test your endurance while refreshing the mind.

Are You Fully Engaged?

Between 1975 and 1990, Mihaly Csikszentmihalyi worked diligently to develop his flow theory. A person is able to reach flow when they are completely engulfed in their work. This intensity results in the absence of time. It seems as if the minutes just fly. Ask yourself, is there ever an activity where flow is achieved? If so, this is likely your area of expertise and perhaps a valuable strength. Activities that obtain our full attention are of interest to us. Pay attention to these moments and look for a commonality within them. Do you experience flow when working on a tedious project? What about during work; do you have those moments of full immersion when attempting to solve a client's problem? Take notice of when you experience flow in order to determine your true strengths.

When it comes to uncovering our weaknesses, the task is less daunting in nature. For the most part, we know what makes us tick and jabs our esteem. However, often times our *kryptonite* is only discovered through trial and error. A compilation of less than pleasing experiences that produced a breakdown in our psyche. Do you notice areas in your life that could use some TLC? Are there aspects of your career that you find increasingly difficult to accomplish? Or, are your interpersonal relationships likened to combat?

In 2009, a poll was taken where participants were instructed to name their 10 strengths and weaknesses. Out of the individuals polled, there were five weaknesses that were consistent throughout the survey. They were:

- Emotionally Reactive

- Inability to Focus

- Balanced Social Skills

- Overthinking

- Lacking Patience

Take A Look at Your Environment

Being a product of your environment is no mere excuse. In fact, the University of Minnesota quoted, *"The environment can influence mood. For example, the results of several research studies reveal that rooms with bright light, both natural and artificial, can improve health outcomes such as depression, agitation, and sleep."* [2] Do you constantly feel rushed when preparing for the day? Do you find it increasingly difficult to locate items within your house? If so, disorganization can be your weakness. Find ways to declutter, clean, and sort your items so that your preparation is fluid.

What Prompts Stress?

In order to conquer your weaknesses head on, you must identify them. Throughout the day, there are various triggers that can result in feelings of distress. Usually, the times when you feel overwhelmed all have a common root cause. Stress is

---

[2] RN, PhD, Kreitzer, Mary Jo (2016): University of Minnesota-What Impact Does the Environment Have on Us?

a tricky emotion that can creep into our mood without warning. When you begin to feel stressed, ask yourself:

- What were the circumstances surrounding this distress?

- Who was around when the stress ensued?

- When did you begin to feel stressed?

- Was it a particular task, activity, image, or conversation that encouraged the stress?

By analyzing when the stress occurred and what prompted it, you can pin point what weakens your energy. Although a small amount of stress can promote productivity, stress on a large level is stifling. It can even inhibit growth.

Analyze Your Response

When contemplating your personal relationships, do you often times encounter conflict? When this occurs, how do you respond? By analyzing your response to negative stimuli, you will better understand what your weakness is. When engaging in certain activities, analyze when they evolve from stimulating to difficult. Perhaps writing detailed passages may be laborious. If so, attention to detail may be your weakness. If having to deal with customers on a daily basis drains your energy, customer service may be your vice. Pay attention to how your body and mind react to various situations in order to correctly identify your weakness.

Emotional intelligence begins with revealing your strengths and weaknesses. They are vital to truly understanding the self on a deeper level. Emotional growth can only occur when the vulnerabilities of the mind are conquered head on. By constantly swimming in the midst of blindness, it can be easy to repress emotions that can result in stagnation. On the contrary, constant exposure to your weaknesses can have a huge impact on your self-confidence. That is why highlighting your strengths is vital to building your self-value. You will push yourself to new limits and open the door for greater opportunities.

Chapter 2:
How to Properly Identify and
Express Your Needs

Maslow's Hierarchy of needs is an excellent blueprint for identifying your needs from primal to complex. Organisms as small as seeds require water in order to survive. The amount of care and attention varies between each plant. However, they each have their own unique needs. We are manufactured in the same manner. In order to live purposeful lives, we have to have our needs met. In fact, individuals in romantic relationships are reportedly happier when they feel that their personal needs are being taken into consideration.

In 1943, Maslow theorized the evolution of needs through categorizing deficiency needs in comparison to growth needs. He believed that in order to move up to higher level thinking, we needed to fulfill our primal needs first. Then, as we begin to adequately meet those needs, we can move up to the next one.[3] He quotes, *At once other (and "higher") needs emerge and these, rather than physiological hungers, dominate the organism. And when these, in turn, are satisfied, again new (and still "higher") needs emerge and so on. This is what we mean by saying that the basic human needs are organized into a hierarchy of relative prepotency.*

---

[3] McLeod, Saul (2017): Maslow's Hierarchy of Needs

When contemplating the legitimacy of his theory, it's safe to conclude that we cannot properly function unless our immediate needs are accurately met. For example, have you tried going to work on an empty stomach? Perhaps without your morning coffee. Your ability to accomplish your goals is likely compromised as you haven't properly fueled your body. However, if you start your day with a nutritious breakfast, you are able to conquer the day with confidence! This same approach should be used when analyzing our everyday needs. By taking care of the important, immediate needs first, everything else will fall in line.

Some examples of complex needs are,

- The need to feel valuable

- The need to feel respected

- The need to be nurtured

- The need to nurture others

- The need for companionship

- The need for a physical connection with someone

- The need for personal space and freedom

- The need to express yourself honestly

As children, we likely encountered situations where our needs were not met emotionally. Perhaps there were occasions of neglect or repressed anger taken place within

the household. If you never truly dealt with those emotions as a child, they could manifest themselves into unhealthy patterns of behavior. For example, if a child was never given the opportunity to express themselves, they may grow up seeking to control everything they encounter. Since they equate a level of anxiety associated with losing control, they create an unhealthy compulsion to manipulate situations in their favor. The danger in not dealing with your needs being met is immense. In fact, anxiety and obsessive-compulsive disorder are actually results of ignored needs over a period of time. The mind is desperately trying to find a way to cope with the unmet need. It is imperative to your health to identify your needs and express them so as to remain healthy and balanced.

How Can I Identify My Needs?

Although the need for shelter, nutrition, and water are instinctual, we cannot survive without a compilation of the three. These needs are engrained in us. In addition to these primal needs, we also have complex desires that must be fulfilled in order to reach a level of satisfaction. These needs span from personal gratification to feeling respected by your partner. The question now is, how can you properly identify those complex needs?

One way to determine your personal needs is to consider where your purpose lies. Perhaps you are working in a stifling job that doesn't allow you to use your skills. Likely, your job is holding you back from reaching your full potential. This absence of fulfillment lies the true nature of your need. A few personal questions to consider are:

- What brings me fulfillment?

- When do I feel valuable?

- Which values are important to me?

- How do I want to be remembered?

The answers to those questions will give you greater insight towards your purpose. Although instances of positivity can reveal our need for value, negative experiences can help to shape how we seek to be treated in the future. Our needs are highly based on emotional reactions. It is the art of determining what you are going to tolerate from another person without compromising yourself. These needs are highly prevalent in our personal relationships. For example, if a woman is dating a man who constantly ignores her expressions of concern, she will no doubt feel unimportant to him. Her need for a partner who values her opinion is not being met. In the future, she may seek a mate who takes her concerns seriously. Some of the basic needs for our personal relationships include a sense of belongingness, affection, acceptance, and intimacy. [4] Out of the various complexities of what we yearn for, respect is considered one of the primary needs that must be met above all else. When this is fulfilled, everything will inevitably fall into place.

When contemplating work, the average person may shutter at the thought. Although their job provides for them monetarily, they may feel used and unhappy. When this occurs, it's important to identify what your needs are in terms of employment and how can you achieve them? Do you yearn to try a different skill? Do you need more flexibility with your schedule? Are you being fairly compensated? Are the members of your team encouraging or draining? Do you feel respected by your superiors? By honestly evaluating the answers to those questions, you will determine what your employment needs are. Then, you can create your plan of action accordingly.

Personal Needs

The fourth tier in Maslow's hierarchy is esteem needs. These can be likened to our self-esteem, confidence, and self-value. The way we perceive ourselves is projected onto the world. In turn, others will treat us accordingly. There are specific personal needs that help us to feel productive and balanced. Some include:

1. Feeling confident in your outward appearance

2. Engaging in activities that are gratifying and showcase out skillset

3. A feeling of worth and achievement

____

[4] McLeod, Saul (2017): Maslow's Hierarchy of Needs

4. An established self-identity

The challenge of identifying and fulfilling our personal needs is the conundrum of the mind. Although we may feel healthy and confident, there is always that glimmer of self-doubt that destroys our esteem. It could be the pretty neighbor upstairs or the genius coder on your team at work. It could also be repressed memories and experiences that left you thinking you were unworthy. Whatever the root, the commonality is a feeling if insecurity. An overwhelming unworthiness that shapes your behavior.

One of the primary ways to conquering feelings of insecurity is to practice self-gratitude. This begins with speaking positive affirmations daily that consist of your physical attributes, accomplishments, and skills. By emphasizing your strong points, you will grow accustomed to speaking highly of yourself. In addition, taking care of your body demonstrates immense gratitude. Engage in physical activities that push your efforts. Reward your body with nutritious foods that will complement your progress. By fulfilling the need to be healthy, you are showing your body that you appreciate it.

The Importance of Expressing Your Needs

Expressing your needs can be compared to a refreshing glass of water on a summer day. The act of orally requesting respect is both refreshing and imperative to survival. However, the *act* of expressing one's needs is often challenging. Many find difficulty with speaking their emotions for a number of reasons. Some may include:

- The inability to properly identify emotions

- An unhealthy fear of other's opinions

- The disdain for appearing vulnerable

- Cultural and environmental factors

- A lack of trust in personal relationships

- Negative previous experiences

- The fear of losing a position, relationship, or reputation

Despite the overall fear surrounding speaking up, the importance of doing so is vital. When you continue to push your personal needs to the back burner, you will begin to notice unhealthy patterns of behavior. In addition, others will use and manipulate you to their advantage. It may seem as if they disregard your value as a human being. As previously mentioned, Obsessive Compulsive Disorder can often times be a result of suppressed needs. When your specific needs aren't being met, you begin to feel an inward anxiety; anger even. If you allow these feelings to continue without treatment, your mind begins to find compulsions to cope with that anxiety. This may result in irrational thoughts, repetitive behavior, and obsessive fixations. The compulsion or intrusive thought isn't the problem, the need being ignored is.

In addition, feeling comfortable expressing your needs will help to improve your quality of life. The old saying, *"Closed mouths don't get fed"* is no downtown-slang. In fact, it can be the difference between happiness and utter misery. By speaking up, you hold the power to changing your future. If others continue to disregard your needs, you have the confidence to leave them behind.

How Can I Express My Needs?

If you have anxiety surrounding orally expressing yourself, your fear isn't invalid. It takes great courage putting yourself out there without truly knowing the consequences. However, there are practical tips you can implement to make the process easier.

1. Pay Attention to Your Approach

The manner in which you speak with someone can have a drastic effect on how they perceive you and the conversation. In fact, it may even alter the likelihood of you getting what you want. This is 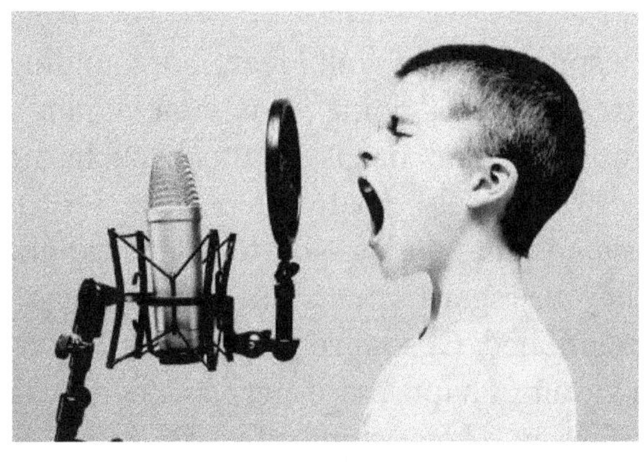 why tone, inflection, volume, and body language are everything. Instead of approaching someone in a combative manner, schedule a time when you are both calm and relaxed. Then, take note of the words you use. Avoid phrases like, "*You never*" or, "*You don't.*" They can come across quarrelsome and argumentative. Instead, focus only on the issue at hand. Be cognizant to leave out blame, explosive vernacular, and trigger words. Simply state the facts and express your feelings with maturity. Here are a few examples to help guide your conversation:

Avoid using language that could cause intense conflict. Some include:

A. This job is draining me physically! I can't take it anymore!

B. You never listen to me! You are so selfish!

C. I'm tired of you always leaving your dirty dishes out! You are so gross!

D. I can't take being in this boring relationship.

Instead, ensure your needs are properly heard and not being lost in accusations.

A. I appreciate working here, but I feel like I am burning out.

B. I have something important to talk about; do you have a few minutes?

C. Let's make a schedule together so we can keep the kitchen clean.

D. Let's go out this weekend and have some fun!

Do you see the distinction between the two sentences? The first group had an overall tone of anger. It was quite accusing and blatantly rude. However, the second set vocalized the need without sounding vindictive.

2. Utilize Written Expressions

If you find it increasingly difficult to gather your thoughts, write them down prior to your conversation. This way, you can release all of your intense emotions on paper while organizing your thoughts. Use this as an opportunity to explain how you are feeling without holding back. You will better understand what your need truly is as opposed to masking it with emotion. Then, when the time comes for you to orally express them, you are able to do so in a concise manner.

3. Use Discretion

Approaching your manager after she just lost a major deal with an important client may not be the best time to discuss your job satisfaction. Timing is everything, especially so when you are addressing an issue. Their current mood could turn a mature conversation into a heated debate. In the end, you may even go without having your needs properly met. Schedule a time when you and your partner are both calm, relaxed, and in a generally good mood. This will vastly improve the quality of your conversation.

Chapter 3:
How to Determine Your Self-Value

As we briefly discussed in the previous chapter, self-value is one of the essential needs to feeling fulfilled and confident. The value of something is usually based on predetermined labels that were created in the past. For example, the Penny is valued at one cent, whereas the Quarter has a value of 25 cents. If you present a child with the option of a penny or quarter, likely they will choose the quarter because it has a greater value. These are fixated prices that assist with economic movement. The beauty behind personal self-value is that you are able to determine your worth. You have full control over setting expectations of behavior from others and yourself.

Have you felt unworthy of love and outward displays of affection from others? Do you feel as if everyone in your environment is smarter, prettier, or more successful than you? Do you feel taken advantage of by others on a regular basis? If so, you may need to work on developing your self-value. A few examples include:

- Constantly putting yourself down in your mind or in front of others

- Intense jealousy and insecurity in relationships

- Taking outrageous risks with little regard for your future

- Allowing disrespect from your romantic partner

- Never believing in your strengths or skills

- An illusion of grandiosity in public

Your primary focus is not on your limitations, but rather, your capabilities when you value yourself. You attempt to avoid compromising situations where your health, reputation, or freedom is at stake. In fact, researchers who study substance abuse agree that individuals who suffer from a low self-value are prone to addiction. An Atlanta recovery center quoted, "The Mental Health and Counseling Center of the University of Texas reported that low self-esteem can lead to lack of development and/or tendency toward drugs or alcohol consumption." [5] Sick individuals may sense this low self-esteem and use it to their advantage. This could result in abuse, manipulation, and a poor quality of life.

Sadly, situational experiences may contribute to an individual's feeling of inadequacy. Perhaps others in their life constantly emphasized their flaws which led them to constantly feeling low. Because these feelings of worthlessness are deeply engrained, the process of reprograming the mind is a challenge. Negative thinking is a learned habit. Therefore, you have the ability to learn how to think positively about yourself. There are a variety of fun and creative ways that you can incorporate into your daily routine in order to boost your

---

[5] Talbott Recovery (2018): Low Self-Esteem and Drug Abuse: What's the Connection?

self-value. What's wonderful about these exercises is that you can start them immediately!

Practice Daily Self-Affirmations

Self-affirmations are medicine for the soul. In fact, neuroscience has found that practicing daily self-affirmations works in conjunction with neuroplasticity. Our brain has the ability to rewire its function through consistent exercises that work to strengthen weak parts of the brain. Since you are reconstructing your brain to go from negative thinking to positive, you are inadvertently rebuilding brain  function. [6] If science says it's true, why not give it a try! Self-affirmations are excellent tools used for boosting self-esteem and really highlighting your strengths. You can begin by orally repeating your affirmations, or document them in a journal.

---

[6] Flint Rehab (2016): The Power of Affirmations for Stroke Recovery (A 3-Step Process Backed by Science)

Many begin by stating their five greatest attributes whether physical or emotional. Each day, they add more to the list with the hopes of diving deeper within the self. An example looks similar to this:

- I am strong and resilient

- I am creative, innovative, and talented

- I am beautiful, and I love my hair

- I am an awesome friend who is always willing to listen

Begin each day by repeating what you love about yourself and what makes you unique. Soon, you will begin to wear your value on your sleeve.

Remove All Negativity from Your Life

When you have a low self-value, you tend to tolerate unhealthy behavior from others. This is caused by feelings of inadequacy and the ignorance of understanding that they deserve more. In order to rebuild your self-value, you have to have the strength to remove all forms of negativity from your life. This may mean changing to a career that values your skills or leaving an unhealthy relationship. Perhaps even changing your circle of associates to uplifting individuals who seek to encourage you. When you remove toxic situations and individuals, you are inadvertently eliminating all forms of disrespect. Although challenging, you will begin to feel better about yourself as you immerse yourself in positivity.

Elevate How You Perceive Yourself

The brain has the unique ability to rewire itself and alter bad habits. It's easy to make a list of your strong suits, but it's quite challenging to start believing them. Take the way you view yourself to the next level. Change the way you view yourself by not allowing your subconscious thoughts to disrespect you. In essence, prove to yourself the legitimacy of your affirmations. If you truly believe you are the greatest coder on your team, own it! Strive to become indispensable. Become responsible for your thoughts and take ownership of the fact that you can control negativity.

Challenge Yourself

A low self-value is the consequence of remaining stagnant. The endless stream of negative thoughts have subsequently held you back from leaving your comfort zone. It's almost as if negative thinking is home, and the entry to self-actualization is galaxies away. Fortunately, you have the power to build your own spaceship and reach those galaxies. Heighten your skill set by trying to elevate your skills. Push yourself beyond your normal boundaries in order to really see a change. Engage in activities that require you to think, pay attention to detail, and evoke a little fear. By doing so, you will begin to see the beauty in your capabilities.

Accept Responsibility and Seek Forgiveness

When dealing with deeply rooted self-esteem issues, likely they stem from severe experiences of hurt. Accept responsibility for the fact that you allowed someone else to mold your perception. Then, seek to forgive the situation, person, or outcome. This may be a challenge initially but attempt to adjust your perception. Was the person who made you feel poorly about yourself dealing with mental health issues? Perhaps they had a low self-value and projected it on others. When you strive to think about them with an empathetic tone, you may start to understand the validity of their illness. This will make it easier for you to forgive and ultimately forget.

By accepting responsibility, you aren't blaming yourself for the negative actions of others. Rather, you are controlling how to react to the situation. If someone is constantly putting you down, you have the power to block their negativity and place emphasis on your value.

Vocalizing Your Feelings and Walking Away

By giving undue attention to the behavior of others, you are giving them power. In essence, you are showing them that you are okay with how they are treating you. Have the power to defend yourself and vocalize those feelings. If someone is constantly belittling you or pointing out your flaws, let them know how that makes you feel. If they choose to disregard your feelings, have the power to walk away from the conversation. In severe cases, removing the person from your life all together is necessary. The key to remember is that you have the control to dominate your emotions. Don't give someone else the power to change they beauty you possess.

Disregard Titles

One of the primary sources of developing a low self-value is this looming air of superiority. Individuals place so much emphasis on their salary, job title, and social status, that they begin to disregard the inner person. Perhaps you feel ashamed of your job position and even the amount of money you make. If this occurs, stop feeling ashamed and start finding meaning in your position. No matter the job title, your work is valuable. Imagine what your career or job would do without your hard work. Seek to find a sense of purpose in your position.

Eliminate Comparisons

Comparing yourself to others can greatly impact your self-value. When you consistently compare your success with someone else's, it can have an impact on your self-esteem. Instead of emphasizing someone else's strong points, why not focus on what makes you special. What do you have that no one else does? What talents, goals, aspirations, and personality traits make you unique? Comparing yourself is counterproductive. Take action and begin to see the value in yourself.

Understanding your self-value requires action and patience. The results of your hard work will not happen overnight. Rather, you will begin to slowly build your value into something indestructible. Carrying negative weight around is heavy. It results in a never-ending cycle of attempting to please others. When you let go of comparisons, societal expectations, and low self-esteem, you will truly enjoy the freedom associated with self-love. Start practicing these tips today and you will begin to see a major shift in your perspective.

Chapter 4:
Unique Ways to Identify Goals
and Actually Meet Them

Goal setting is imperative to self-success. In order to progress, there needs to be an opportunity for growth. Often times, setting goals can be quite overwhelming especially when there is a lack of direction. Researchers Gary Latham and partner Edwin Locke developed the goal setting theory in 1975. Through their findings, they developed the thesis, "Working towards a determinate goal would lead to a higher level of task interest than would the case with an abstract goal such as do your best." [7] When we are given specific levels of achievement to reach, we are more likely to meet them with enthusiasm and success. It can be likened to the direction, "Go climb the nearest mountain" versus, "Hike to the top of Mt. Everest in only a week." The second gives a timeline, destination, and action whereas the

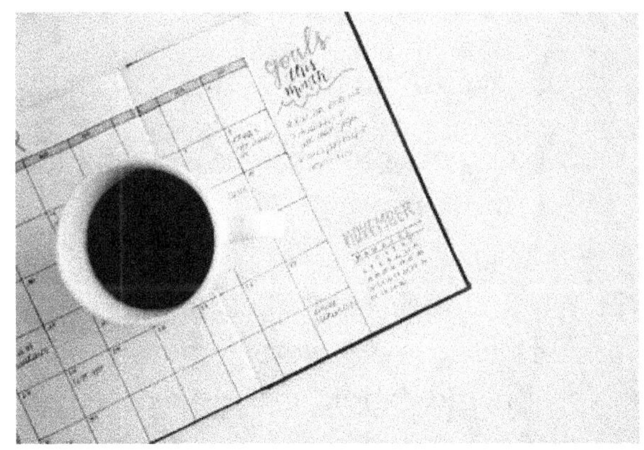

---

[7] Miner, John (2005) "Organizational Behavior 1: Essential Theories of Motivation and Leadership", p. 160

first isn't specific. It doesn't prompt you to actually go out and accomplish the task.

The Importance of Being Detailed with Your Goals

In our everyday lives, we have the opportunity to set valuable goals for ourselves. The challenge with setting a goal comes when the sense of urgency isn't felt. We may want to make a valuable change, but if we don't approach it with great urgency, the likelihood of us being able to accomplish it is slim. Let's consider a few examples of broad goals and detailed. Then, we will discuss which evoke feelings of excitement and motivation.

1. I want to run a 5k race

2. I am going to save $1,000 by June 1st so I can quit my job and pursue freelancing.

3. I am going to wake up at 5 am every day so I can go to the gym and lose 10 pounds by summer.

4. I want to get a new job

5. I want to pursue acting

6. I am going to practice drawing for 20 minutes a day, so I can improve on my skills.

Did you notice the distinction between the sentences? Numbers 1, 4, and 5 were rather broad and boring. They gave no specific indication of the purpose behind the goal. Nor did they have a suggested deadline to meet. Do you think that person was able to meet their goals? More than likely they fell short. On the contrary, numbers 2,3, and 6 were specific, time focused, and they gave a valuable outcome. What's your reason behind your current goal? This reason is your motivating force that should be a part of your focus. When you give yourself a specific endpoint, this motivates you to continue working.

How to Identify Goals

When you take an introspective look at your life, do you see any areas for improvement? Do you wish to change something about yourself or your situation in order to live a happier life? If so, use these observations as the blueprint for your goals. This takes a level of personal honesty and evaluation on your part. You have to be your own greatest critic in order to find potential areas for growth. Here are a few valuable questions to consider:

- Could I improve my diet?

- Could I engage in active exercise at least three times per week?

- Am I pushing myself in my job?

- How can I improve my freelance business and build clientele?

One effective way to accomplish this is to write down different aspects of your life that you wish to change. Maybe divide it between work, family life, social, and personal. Then, write the corresponding question with each section. Think deeply about each portion of your life and how much effort you are putting towards it.

Are You Prepared to Sacrifice?

Atonement is a biblical term used to describe the sacrificial act of giving up something in order to receive a higher blessing. The bible book of Leviticus is filled with stories surrounding the ancient practice of animal sacrificing in an attempt to please their god. While this practice is shunned today, we still carry out the principle when hoping to receive success. When embarking on a journey of self-improvement, are you willing to give up your past habits in order to achieve something great?

Francesca Righetti and co-authors from an Amsterdam University sought to test the correlation between sacrifices, gut instincts, and relationships. They believed that our gut intuition directs our steps towards making a sacrifice. They began this study by gathering together a group of participants and their significant others. They were instructed to approach strangers on the street and ask them rather shameful and outlandish questions. The partners self-dictated how they would manage their approach and divide the work. Previously, the participants were graded on their impulse control which served as valuable data for proving the theory. Throughout the exercise, the individuals who demonstrated a high level of self-control were more likely to ask the embarrassing questions and take on the majority of the work. Whereas, individuals who acted on impulse divided the work evenly. [8] In summation, if we demonstrate a high level of impulse control, we are more likely to sacrifice our happiness for that of our partner.

---

[8] Desar, Leonora (2013): The Truth About Sacrifice

What does this research have to do with goal setting? One of the most important relationships we have is with yourself. We have to sacrifice a number of desires in order to reach our full potential. Since we discovered that impulse control has a great effect on our ability to actually sacrifice our happiness, it's of value to consider working on our impulsivity. Do you tend to binge watch your favorite series for hours as opposed to studying for a test? Do you reach for that yummy cupcake when you are hoping to lose weight? These tiny impulses within our personality are a hinderance to meeting goals. One way to work on impulsivity is to implement the infamous "stop, drop, and roll" theory to your weakness. Fire, in this case, is the impulsive and ravenous element seeking to stifle our progress. By stopping, you are preventing the fire from spreading. When you drop to the floor, you are taking the first step towards putting the fire out. Then, rolling is taking the needed action towards completely eliminating the fire and seeking assistance. When you are presented with the desire to give into your temptations, immediately stop and think about your goal. Then, drop your immediate reaction to bring the temptation into your life. Finally, roll your focus onto something productive; an action that will help you to get closer to your goal.

Integrative Ways to Remained Focused

Vision boards are excellent tools used to organize goals, thought processes, and motivation. The beauty of these projects is that you can unleash your creativity and create something of value for you. You can glue or pin quotes, photos of your goal, or even picture of you carrying out your dream in order to boost motivation. By keeping this board in a viable place, you are forcing yourself to look at those goals daily. This serves as a helpful reminder to take action throughout the day and make good decisions.

Another great way to meet your goals is to set milestones in between your final destination. For example, if your goal is to lost x number of pounds in a month, divide up each week with a specific goal. Perhaps by the end of week one, your goal is to lose three pounds. Week two, you hope to lose four, and so forth. This eliminates any room for feeling overwhelmed. It will also boost your confidence in that you will actually see what you are capable of. When you notice small changes, it will move you to keep going towards the big one.

Writing down your goals and milestones are excellent ways to remain organized. In today's technologically advanced society, applications are built daily to assist with productivity. Set reminders that go off at a certain time that will keep you on task. Set deadlines for yourself in writing for mental clarity. This will help you to treat your goals with seriousness. Provide small rewards for yourself as you continue to make progress. Positive reinforcement has been used to keep people motivated and excited about engaging in challenging activities.

Speak Your Goals Out Loud

Although we are our greatest motivating force, those in our support system can be valuable sources of encouragement. When you tell others about your goals, they can help you to stay on course. Through constructive criticism, they can hold you accountable for your actions. In addition, they may be able to provide resources to assist you in meeting your goal. In addition, your support system will understand the sacrifices you are making. They won't feel offended or taken aback when you are suddenly behaving in a different manner. Their trust, insight, and understanding will help you to remain focused on your journey.

Goal setting doesn't have to be an overwhelming fret of endless tasks and strict routines. In fact, goal setting can actually be quite creative and fun. It gives you the valuable opportunity to be able to improve yourself while strengthening your abilities. If you want to live the live you've always dreamt of, you have to put in the necessary work in order to achieve your goals. By holding yourself to a higher standard, you are essentially setting yourself up for a lifetime of excitement and success.

Chapter 5:
Excellent Ways to Challenge Yourself

One tech savvy individual is greatly inspired by the quietness of nature. For a week, he secludes himself within a hidden cabin far away from the buzzing distractions of daily life. He has absolutely no contact with friends and family members and he limits himself to only two meals a day. During this time, he spends 18 hours working; brainstorming new ideas, concepts, and innovations. This Mountain man is no expert survivalist; he is none other than Bill Gates. [9]

Do you think Mr. Gates particularly enjoys roughing it in the woods as opposed to relaxing in his multi-billion-dollar estate? No doubt, he would probably prefer spending valuable time with his friends and family. Besides, he's already one of the world's greatest influencers. Why does he continue to push himself? The answer lies in his inability to forget his purpose. Bill Gates could rightly hire someone to do the thinking for him! Instead, he continues to challenge himself despite unsurmountable success. His passion to create fresh ideas motivates him to continue striving towards his next goal. This is what separates him from others in his bracket.

---

[9] Anderson, Debbie (2016): Extreme Ways Brilliant People Challenge Themselves

Challenging yourself keeps your mind focused, motivated, and refreshed. It creates new heights for the mind to reach, which enforces excitement. Challenge is the beginning of improvement. When faced with difficult situations, you are in effect transforming yourself into something indestructible. There are creative ways to challenge yourself that don't involve retreating into the woods alone.

Ask for Constructive Criticism

The last thing we typically want to hear is what we're doing wrong. However, constructive criticism is far from being hurtful. Norman Vincent Peale once quoted, *"The*  *trouble with most of us is that we would rather be ruined by praises than saved by criticism."* In popular culture, these individuals are referred to condescendingly as "yes-men." These are the ones who worship celebrities even while witnessing their demise. They refrain from telling them the truth of their outlandish actions as a means to avoid conflict. These individuals are not limited to the rich and famous. In fact, we all encounter these yes-men and women on a daily basis. The individuals who hold back from encouraging you and watch aimlessly as you burn. However, real associates who want to see you grow, are not afraid to hold back on the constructive criticism. This poses a great challenge to our ego, but the result is evolution. Ask for feedback on ideas, projects, or even personality traits. Then, you will understand specific areas of improvement.

Seek Knowledge Through Reading

Reading and researching compelling topics will give you greater insight into the thinking process of others. Often times, we are so accustomed to our perspective, we begin to believe our way is the only correct path. However, when you dive into motivational autobiographies, scientific novels, and even self-help books, you will begin to see how others overcame challenges. In addition, this form of knowledge seeking will broaden your intelligence as you begin to learn new things. This is a great yet rewarding challenge.

The internet is full of free classes that can teach interested ones the basics of all sorts of topics. What's interesting is that some college professors even post their class lectures online and free of charge! You have the opportunity to soak up challenging information that can help you to advance in your career or pursue your dreams.

Listen to Podcasts

If reading is time consuming, podcasts are excellent tools that provide information on a wide variety of topics. Much like reading, you are able to hear the different perspectives of others. Podcast hosts spend a grand amount of time researching their topics so as to provide accurate and interesting information. A few fantastic categories to consider are psychology, current events, history, and even neuroscience. You'll be surprised how much information you can retain through listening!

Engage in Unique Hobbies

An independent film showcased the challenging yet rewarding feeling of learning how to knit. Terminally ill cancer patients engaged in this activity through the means of a support group. Although they were battling the various obstacles associated with cancer, they used knitting as a means to cope with the anxiety. They pursued something challenging despite being faced with one of the most challenging illnesses of our time. Have you considered joining an art, yoga, or spinning class? Getting out of your comfort zone will assist with building new skills you were previously unaware of. The act of embarking on a new hobby will challenge your mind to take on unfamiliar tasks.

Speak Your Truth

Do you find sharing your personal story to be quite scary? What about in front of an audience? A majority of us would shutter at the thought. However, public speaking is an excellent way to practice speaking your written words in an organized and enthusiastic manner. The ability to face a crowd and deliver a speech without apprehension is invigorating.

Travel Near and Travel Far

Mark Twain once quoted, "Travel is fatal to prejudice, bigotry, and narrow-mindedness." Traveling to a far away country is a fun and creative way to challenge yourself. Visiting a land that speaks a language totally different from your own will encourage you to leap from your comfort zone in order to get around. In addition, traveling far is a great lesson in humility. Imagine living in a country where you cannot get your basic needs met because of a language barrier. This may help you to have more compassion when dealing with foreigners in your land. Embracing a different culture educates you on their traditions, customs, and cuisine. By engulfing yourself completely in another culture, you are putting yourself out there to experiment new and exciting things.

Often times traveling far can be a challenge to our wallets. Although traveling to an exotic place is ideal, you can find a hidden gem buried in your backyard. Explore what your city has to offer. Try new restaurants, associate with a new crowd, and explore areas of your town you have never seen. You may gain inspiration right outside of your front yard.

Make Human Connections with New People

It's simple to sit behind a phone or laptop and "like" or comment on those in your networks photos. As yourself, how well do you really know these people? Sure, you enjoy looking at what they choose to show, but is it real? The art of making human connections through effective communication may be *so last year*. However, that's what makes it an exciting challenge! Push yourself to meet new people, in person. Carry on purposeful conversations with those you meet by asking valuable questions and making eye contact. You never know who you may connect and build a friendship with.

Begin Your Day Earlier

Waking up earlier than usual can boost your productivity. By starting your day just 30 minutes earlier, you are able to prepare your obligations, meditate, and even exercise! We all understand why waking up earlier is considered a challenge. In all honesty, the bed is like our safe haven from the day. However, push yourself to leave your literal comfort zone and get moving! You may be blown away by all that you can accomplish!

Challenging yourself is a refreshing way to gain more insight into your capabilities. The beauty of overcoming obstacles is that it builds your resiliency. When you find yourself accomplishing one difficult feat, you will want to continue doing more. This contagious feeling will assist you on your journey of growth.

Chapter 6:
Integrative Ways to Reach
Self-Actualization

At the height of Maslow's hierarchy of needs was the illustrious self-actualization. The creme de la creme of the self. The dictionary definition is, "The realization or fulfillment of one's talents and potentialities, especially considered as a drive or need present in everyone." The psychological definition is, "Realizing personal potential, self-fulfillment, seeking personal growth and peak experiences." [10] In order to reach self-actualization, you have to work towards your full potential. By being all you can be, you are experiencing the beauty of life with great strength. There are valuable tips and tricks available to help you to reach your full potential and live your best life. Let's consider a few.

Practice Mindfulness

Abraham Maslow placed great emphasis on living in the moment and experiencing flow. Mindfulness is the practice of engaging in the moment without undue fear of the future or past. The impact this mentality has on feeling self-actualized is that it eliminates any room for anxiety. Since fear can prevent us from reaching our full potential, it is vital to creating a

---

[10] McLeod, Saul (2017) : Maslow's Hierarchy of Needs

healthy absence from it. Some examples of mindfulness in practice are,

- Meditating in a quiet space

- Deep breathing exercises

- Journaling for mental clarity

- Practicing gratitude

Implement Moral Ideals of Self-Development

Popular blogging platforms connect self-development with productivity. Although accomplishing tasks and remaining motivated are excellent tools for self-improvement, many articles lack mentioning a moral code. The greatest measure of another person is their ability to express kindness towards others. Qualities such as integrity, honesty, and diligence all encompass what it means to be a decent person. Living to your greatest potential doesn't equate to making millions of dollars and acquiring material possessions. Rather, it is your ability to remain humble despite grand accolades. It is your passion to create rather than your need to sell. By taking great pride in your character, you are truly living to your fullest potential. You will gain the respect of others while living with a clear conscious.

Saying Goodbye to the Ego

Sigmund Freud spoke about the id, ego, and superego in his 1923 theories. He explains, "The ego is 'that part of the id which has been modified by the direct influence of the external world."[11] The ego is like a slave to the primal id; jumping at any opportunity to fulfill its wishes. While the id operates on a purely instinctual level, the ego tries its best to consider the opinions of others and societal norms when making a decision. This is referred to as the reality principle. In fact, Freud compared this id, ego relationship to a horseback rider. He explains, "The ego is 'like a man on horseback, who has to hold in check the superior strength of the horse." [12] Since the ego works aimlessly to please the id, often times the reality principle falls short of success. When this happens, anxiety ensues which unearths a host of coping, defense mechanisms used to make the anxiety disappear. [13]These defense mechanisms can come in the form of anger, repressed emotions, and depression. They may even result in unhealthy compulsions or obsessions. In order to live life to your fullest potential, you have to rid yourself of unhealthy habits that are used ad Band-Aids. This includes letting go of the hurt, confronting your inner demons, and letting things beyond your control be. By doing so, you will experience the insurmountable freedom that is incomparable.

Eat Healthy and Nutritious Foods

It is no secret that the foods we consume play a major role in our mental health. For example, researchers have shown that anxiety begins in the stomach. Foods high in fatty carbohydrates, or processed sit within the stomach and has an adverse effect on the digestive tract system. The toxins are then released into the body which contributes to the onset of

---

[11] Freud, Sigmund (1923) p. 25

[12] Freud, Sigmund (1923) p.15

[13] McLeod, Saul (2016): Id, Ego and Superego

anxious feelings. Probiotics and live bacteria can help with cleansing the stomach while purifying the mind. If you eat a healthy, balanced, and nutritious diet, the likelihood of experiencing anxiety and negative thinking will disappear.

In addition, engaging in active exercises regularly will help to release serotonin into the body. This hormone is responsible for mood regulation and overall happiness. Also, working out demonstrates gratitude for your body. You will have more energy to devote towards your activities which will help you to feel productive and fulfilled. Seek to take care of your mind, body, and soul in order to live to your fullest potential.

Allow Yourself to be Free

Self-actualization relies heavily on creative influences. Many artists attribute their greatest works to their unapologetic style. This immense freedom separated them from common artists of their time. Are you allowing yourself to be free and live the life you want? The opinions of others may weigh heavily on your mind. This weight can be so burdensome, it impacts your daily decisions. The problem with this way of thinking is that you are doing a disservice to yourself. You have the responsibility to create your own happiness without the pressure of considering others. If you decided to live your entire life by the guidelines of someone else, you will never reach your full potential. Your uniqueness will disappear into an abyss. Allow yourself the privilege of making your own decisions especially if it greatly impacts your future. Listen to your intuition and take action towards claiming your control!

There is great joy found in the creative process. The artist is able to freely paint his or her emotions without worrying about an outcome. Do you approach situations in a like manner? Sure, we all have instinctual patterns that guide our decisions. However, are you truly living in the moment and acting with your emotions? If you decide to stop engaging with fear and start living with freedom, you will begin to feel the weight of the world being lifted off of your shoulders.

Think in Verbs

It is easy to sit and brainstorm different ideas daily. However, where is all of that energy going if it isn't moving you towards success? When you begin to think in action words, you will begin to take steps towards reaching your goal. This encourages the self to do all it can to reach its full potential. Sit down and analyze what you are saying to yourself daily. Is it positive? Uplifting? Do you often criticize yourself without limits? Surely, this mentality isn't productive. Instead, use action words when facing limitations. Instead of saying, "This is impossible," rephrase that sentence with, "let me research how to get this done." By doing so, you will see a great improvement in your attitude and productivity.

Take into Account Opposing Perspectives

We live in a very divided society. One view is starkly different from the other, and when confronted, the exchange can be brutal. Although everyone is entitled to their own opinion, it's important to seek understanding even when it directly opposes your faith. Being an open-minded person involves a level of maturity. It is separating emotions and focusing on the facts. It is the highest level of emotional intelligence because it relies heavily on empathy. This is the ability to understand why or how another person can feel the way they do. Perhaps research a topic that is contradictory to your personal beliefs. Read personal accounts, research papers, and even statistics that define their mentality. Then, try to understand their position without shifting your stance. This will open your mind to new possibilities and help you to understand the differences of others.

Be Firm in Your Decisions

One of the primary indications of a person with a low self-esteem is their inability to stick to one decision. They allow the opinions of others to quickly shift their initial choice to an opposing one. When you are self-actualized, you trust your intuition. You understand that you are responsible enough to make adequate decisions for your life. Many people find it quite difficult to separate what others want from them and their own desires. One key way to manage this stress is to practice saying no to previous obligations. Initially, this may seem uncomfortable, but your self-esteem will thank you. Soon, you will begin to see how easy it is to put yourself first. In addition, there is a solid reason behind why you feel the way you do about certain situations. Allow that to be your guiding force and not the looming opinions of others. By doing so, you will find great power and strength in yourself.

Never Be Afraid to Defend Yourself

Toxic people have a goal of hurting those around them. They seek out vulnerable prey in order to make them feel inadequate. The popular phrase, "If you don't stand for something, you will fall for anything" directly relates to feeling self-actualized. When ignorant people offend you in an outlandish manner, don't be afraid to speak up. Defend yourself with honor so that others understand your self-respect. Use this as an opportunity to educate others on their lack of knowledge as opposed to setting them straight. By doing so, you may have a great effect on their perspective.

Chapter 7:
How to Manage Your Emotions and Build Lasting Relationships

Emotional management is the ability to regulate your emotions even when provoked. This is a vital life skill because there are various opportunities for conflict that present themselves daily. The way we react to emotional distress can stem back to our familial structure. Perhaps you witnessed verbal or physical abuse within the home and this impacted the way you deal with anger. Maybe you grew up in an extremely conservative home where emotions were never discussed. These social roles all play a vital role in your interactions with others. Even familial structures have a large impact on how you make connections, interact with others, and maintain friendships. For example, when children witness the divorce of their parents, they are more likely to develop negative views towards relationships than children who didn't experience a childhood divorce. Children of divorced parents

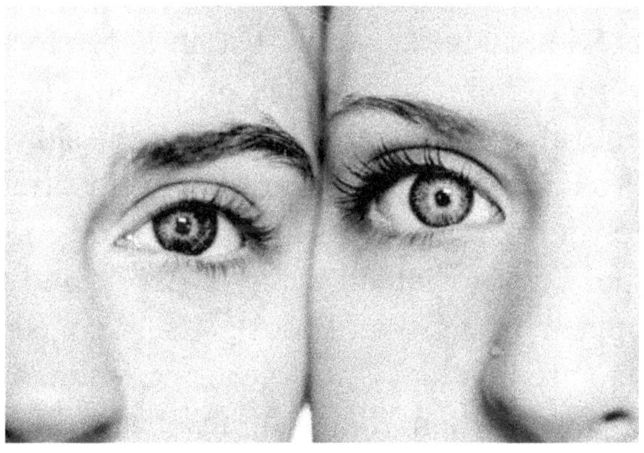

are accustomed to seeing their parent walk away from an unhappy situation. Therefore, it is easier for them to leave a relationship behind and pursue something else. The act of building lasting relationships requires an in-depth look at your past relationships and carefully analyzing areas of improvement.

Issues with Trust

Friendships and relationships are built on the value of trust. One person believes that their partner or friend has their best interests at heart. Likely, they know that they wouldn't do anything to compromise the relationships. However, when a person experiences a pattern of distrustful situations, they begin to look at others with skepticism. In addition, parental roles play a huge role in how we trust others. If you experienced a parent leaving or dissolving the parent-child relationship, likely, you will have trouble trusting others. Since this is such a major, deeply rooted issue, it's quite challenging to break the cycle.

In order to regain your trust with others is to confront your past and make peace with it. Acknowledge the individuals who previously broke your trust and seek forgiveness. By doing so, you are relieving yourself of the burden as opposed to holding onto it. If necessary, have a discussion with the person who broke your trust in order to gain closure. After closing the door to your past, be picky about who you choose to allow into your life. Look for small signs of deceit and turn away when they appear. When you choose wisely concerning your associates, you are less likely to experience feelings of hurt. Finally, learn to love. When the past has brought about insurmountable pain, it is easy to take it out on others. The problem with that mentality is that you are eliminating people who could prove to be good friends. When you find trustworthy people, don't push them away with insecurity. Rather, take it slow and embrace the friendship. You would hate to miss out on something valuable.

Issues with Building Connections

Social anxiety can play a major role in why making friends may be difficult. Sure, putting yourself out there and opening up to others may be scary, but it's worth the risk. When dealing with social anxiety, one of the best ways to eliminate fear is to simply conquer it head on. Make yourself talk to others, go to events, and socialize. When you continue to make excuses for yourself, you will never grow. Cut negative thinking out cold turkey and communicate with others. By doing so, you are showing yourself that fear no longer has a residency in your body. Rather, you are acting on what you want by making friends.

Begin by finding a solid connection with someone. This can be done by exchanging commonalities, sharing experiences, or simply engaging in small talk. Humor is one excellent way to breaking the ice and turning an uncomfortable situation into something enjoyable. The key here is to remember that people are just people. There is beauty in not taking yourself too seriously. Enjoy the moment and take the pressure off of meeting new people. Besides, it is meant to be a fun experience.

Issues with Emotional Regulation

Individuals who are labeled as moody, often have deeply ingrained insecurities that haven't been conquered. This could result in explosive expressions of anger, sadness, or even manic behavior. Does this sound familiar? If so, gaining control over your emotions is challenging, but attainable. Begin by confronting your insecurities head on. This may require deep, self-analyzation with the help of a trained professional. Then, begin to notice when your moods begin to shift. This could be a huge sign as to why you are feeling annoyed. Avoid certain triggers like large groups, particular individuals, and situational occurrences. Finally, be honest with those around you concerning your condition. Sure, you may experience moments of intense lows, but you also experience exciting highs.

One way to control your emotional response is to practice thinking prior to behaving. This requires self-control especially if one is prone to being impulsive. However, by learning how to slow down before you make a decision, you are able to better control your response. For example, if a person disrespects you in public by saying harsh words, what would you ordinarily do? Likely, you would engage in a very public argument. However, when you think before you behave, you may realize that the person throwing those insults at you is truly sick. They have their own insecurities to work out. Therefore, by using empathy, you are able to walk away from the situation with dignity. This takes a great amount of practice, but the results are worth it. You will be filled with mental clarity and a soundness of mind.

Develop Positive Coping Strategies

When we explode or allow our emotions to get the best of us, usually we lack the ability to develop proper coping strategies. When we feel hurt, betrayal, or offense, it is normal to retreat to old habits that may be unhealthy. Some rely on smoking, drinking, or even ignoring the issue all together. While these may prove to be an immediate stress relief, the results are temporary. It is important to develop positive ways to cope with emotions so as not to cause yourself or others harm. First, it is imperative that you find the root cause of your emotions. Issues with anxiety could be a result of a repressed fear. Anger could occur due to a past experience along with a lack of trust. When you identify the root cause, you are able to tackle it head on.

Positive coping strategies are means of comfort that make you feel better while building your confidence. These may include:

- Creative activities that refocus your energy such as cooking, painting, or drawing.

- Writing your feelings down in a journal

- Speaking your emotions to others in a calm manner

- Seeking professional assistance through a counselor or psychologist

There are various activities to engage in that will help you to release stress without harming yourself. Find those activities and use them as your safe-space when times get stressful.

Be the Friend You Would Love to Have

As humans, we are natural receivers. We may place great emphasis on what others are doing or not doing for us. The problem with that thinking is that it doesn't hold us accountable for our actions. In a sense, you are telling yourself that everyone should cater to your needs and wants. If that's the case, others will surely grow tired of that behavior. In order to attract long lasting associates, you have to project what you want onto others. For example, when a friend calls you wanting to talk, do you rush them off of the phone because you are tired? Or, do you take the time out of your day to listen to their issues? The answer will determine what kind of friend you are. People are attracted to kindness and they will reciprocate that when the time comes. Work on building your social interactions by cultivating qualities such as:

1. Selflessness

2. Trustworthiness

3. The ability to listen

4. Empathy and Care

5. Kindness and gratitude

Don't Be Afraid to Seek Help

Emotional regularity is a result of a healthy mind and body. When your mind is in an unhealthy state, naturally your emotions will be all over the place. Certain brain imbalances can contribute to mood swings, anger management, and stress. Often times, vitamins and supplements are used to assist with producing mood boosting hormones in the body. Never be afraid to consult with your doctor on medical or holistic ways to improve your moods. Many vitamin companies specialize in advocating for natural means of healing. In addition, licensed therapists are trained to assist with mood and behavior. They are able to uncover past issues of trauma that could contribute to your mood. Never be afraid to seek their help as there is no shame in self-improvement.

Controlling your emotions goes hand in hand with building lasting relationships. It is quite difficult to keep people in your life if your emotions are constantly going up and down. If you are seeking to build lasting connections, begin by confronting your inner demons. Establish negative habits and seek to dissolve them. Instead, replace those unhealthy habits with positive ones. This could mean seeking professional help, taking supplements or medication, and leaving your comfort zone. The challenge is mighty, but the results are worth the work. Work on your self-confidence in order to be a valuable friend to others. By doing so, you will see the fruits of your labor. Others will naturally be drawn to your demeanor which helps you to have a meaningful life.

Conclusion

Thank for making it through to the end of *Emotional Intelligence: A Beginner's Guide to Understanding Emotions, Raising Your EQ and Improving Your Self-Knowledge*, let's hope it was informative and able to provide you with all of the tools you need to achieve your goals whatever they may be.

It's no secret that life can present obstacles that may seem utterly unbearable. Issues with relationships, self-esteem, and even career choices are all looming reminders of what we are not doing. Despite these challenges, we are composed of instinctual urges that push us to reach our full potential. It is our hope that by reading this e-book and following the information provided that you will reach your full potential and begin to live the life you were meant to live! Although tough, you are capable of becoming in-tuned with your emotions and building your mental strength.

The next step is to share the information found in this e-book with friends and family members. Encourage them to download a copy so as to further enhance their emotional intelligence. It is our hope that everyone can eventually reach self-actualization within their daily lives.

Finally, if you found this book useful in any way, a review on Amazon is always appreciated!